BROKEN SYMMETRY

BROKEN SYMMETRY

David Citino

Ohio State University Press
Columbus

**Library of Congress
Cataloging-in-Publication Data**

Citino, David, 1947–
    Broken symmetry / David Citino.
        p.   cm.
    ISBN 0-8142-0730-8 (cloth :alk. paper).—
    ISBN 0-8142-0731-6 (pbk. : alk. paper)
    I.   Title.
    PS3553.I86B76   1997
    811'.54—dc21   96-37496
                                              CIP

Text and cover design by Donna Hartwick.
Cover photograph courtesy of Kirk Borne
(Space Telescope Science Institute) and
NASA.
Type set in Palatino and Futura.
Printed by Braun-Brumfield, Inc.,
Ann Arbor, Michigan.

The paper used in this publication meets the
minimum requirements of the American Na-
tional Standard for Information Sciences—
Permanence of Paper for Printed Library
Materials. ANSI Z39.48-1992.

9 8 7 6 5 4 3 2 1

Acknowledgments

American Literary Review: "Whole Wheat, Decaf Black, a Morbid Curiosity"

Beloit Poetry Journal: "Prognosis," "To Robert"

Birmingham Poetry Review: "Grandfather Outshines the Ancient Greeks"

Centennial Review: "A Matter of Perspective"

Chariton Review: "Your Dream House"

Cincinnati Poetry Review: "Meditation on the Three Forms of Tongue Protrusion"

Cream City Review: "Sister Mary Appassionata Announces the Winning Project in the Eighth-Grade Science Fair: Our Good Friends the Insects"

Denver Quarterly: "The Dancing of the Bees, the Progress of Multiple Sclerosis," "Fireflies"

Florida Review: "Real Man Delivers an Anti-Pastoral to the Columbus, Ohio, Chamber of Commerce"

Hollins Critic: "Yes, They Had No Tomatoes"

Italian Americana: "The Bottom Line"

Kansas Quarterly: "In Bavaria, Two Vietnamese Beaten by Skinheads while Onlookers Cheer"

Laurel Review: "Potato," "Sister Mary Appassionata to the Chamber of Commerce: Remains of Earliest Hominid Discovered in Ruins of Atlantis under Lake Erie"

The Literary Review: "On Poetry as Punishment"

New England Review: "The House of Pain"

New Letters: "Clown Fish"

New Virginia Review: "Cold, Cold Poem"

Nightsun: "The Girl Who Made the Stars"

The Ogalala Review: "Broken Symmetry," "'Large Bear Deceives Me'"

Ohio Poetry Review: "Sister Mary Appassionata, Marriage Counselor"

The Ohio Review: "Sister Mary Appassionata Chases the Wind"

Onthebus: "Spring Picnic with Newton, Sudden Storm"

Poems & Plays: "The War between Cookbooks and Diet Books"
Poet & Critic: "The Reckoning"
Poetry: "Smelling the Snow"
Poetry East: "Coach"
Prairie Schooner: "Augustine, Aquinas, a Major League Team,"
  "Gathering the Dear Sweet Dead," "The Land of Atrophy." Re-
  printed by permission. Copyright 1995 University of Nebraska
  Press.
River City (formerly *Memphis State Review*): "Sister Mary
  Appassionata on the History of Madness"
River Styx: "The Art of Hummingbirds"
Salmagundi: "Fra Lippo Lippi Invents a New Halo," "The Other White
  Meat," "The Spirit of Competition"
The Southern Review: "At the Well-Endowed Museum; Or, Curse of
  the Mummy's Tomb"
Texas Review: "Homage to the Undertaker"
Voices in Italian Americana: "On the Proposition That a Nation Gets
  the Cuisine It Deserves"
West Branch: "New Poem," "Sister Mary Appassionata Explicates a
  Graffito for the Eighth-Grade Boys," "Sister Mary Appassionata on
  the Excommunication of the Locusts"

☽

for every student

☾

CONTENTS

III. THE EXCOMMUNICATION OF THE LOCUSTS

IV. CURSE OF THE MUMMY'S TOMB

I.

The Land of Atrophy

GRANDFATHER OUTSHINES THE ANCIENT GREEKS

How many antique ones still lie
in the stony soil of Magna Graecia—
the family's starting place at Italy's end—
jaws clenched tight on a gold coin

to bribe Charon or an Ivy archaeologist
to carry them over the river of hell?
Grandfather, too, bides his time,
on his back in the weatherless dark

of Holy Cross Cemetery, dressed
for eternity in a white Sears shirt—
size 32 sleeves and 15½ neck—
that clip-on tie, favorite suit

of blue serge—creases running true
even after fifteen years, lapels
wide as baby angel wings—the head
from which wisdom poured anointed

with Vitalis and Old Spice,
false teeth still so bright they'd
glitter and shine like burnished coins
if there were the slightest light.

☾

The Spirit of Competition

My little finger shall be
thicker than my father's loins,
Rehoboam, son of Solomon, told
the elders of the northern tribes.

So once I thought, dear Father,
but now truth has leaked out.
Ever the number 2, minor, junior,
I can't hold a candle to you.

In the '40s, before the war,
when you began to sleep
with Mother (for which
I never will forgive you),

a U.S. male averaged
3.40 milliliters a pop, while
today we can squeeze out
only 2.75, a 20% descent,

and in those days you raised
113 million sperm
per milliliter, while I'm lucky
if I can scrape together

60 million, a 40% shortfall.
There are those who'd blame
tainted water tables,
fluorocarbons, DES, PCBs,

but whatever the reason,
I see I'll never be
the man you were, never
stop warning, mourning

my own rash, haughty sons
or fighting this entropy,
the gathering fatigue.
This, this must be the way

the world runs down.

☾

To Robert

What was the difference between us,
beyond my passion for women?
We both held quaint notions of respect
not that far from a *paisan* father's

or *his* peasant father's, a chivalry
that meant opening doors
and walking between a lover
and the street, but a certain night

I actually went down on one knee
to propose to the one who
in fierce dancing would make
other souls, and you, dear friend—

it drove me mad—would cruise
bus stations in Cleveland and Athens
and on your knees open your mouth
to men you didn't know. Beautiful,

you called some of them, so lovely
you'd want to make them sigh.
A mystery, the different ways we went,
so close we were in all things else.

The night that, weeping about some marine,
you came home to the apartment
with crabs, I screamed *Goddamn it,*
How could you? How could you not?

The ways a body dreams itself,
we taught each other—that, and something
about fate, of course. Now other lives
tangle sweetly with my own,

and you're under the grass alone,
the plague having picked you up like
some homicidally beautiful maniac
getting off the bus and looking around

with dark eyes that fix on yours
like the sweet beckoning of night
and both of us too grateful
for the ways of human love

to pray him somewhere far away.

☾

AUGUSTINE, AQUINAS, A MAJOR LEAGUE TEAM

Prayer was a shameless begging for paradise,
If I should die before I wake please take me
to heaven, Augustine's City of God, cold
as church, its pleasures the voyeur's.

I'd gaze on The Man strutting the clouds,
saints yessing him like robed Ali's entourage.
But pudgy, winged retainers meant little
to lower-class me. A land without soul-kissing,

breasts and sighs coming alive in my mouth?
Not a single White Castle? No Percy Sledge,
When a man loves a woman? A town
without trains or an American League team?

Forever for Aquinas was contemplation.
What hell. Eternal Church. Forever School.
I felt a joy where skirts inched up thighs,
while hell was a tumor big as a baseball.

I saw that what I wanted damned me
to coals that barbecued without consuming.
If I wished all time to be unburning
I had to learn to love to hate the world.

If my own mother went north and I south,
she'd be too blissed to mourn my bones
blazing below. If the opposite came to pass—
although nothing could be more unthinkable—

I'd look down on the fire, beautiful
and cruel, writhing her fingers and hair,
that voice crying my name hoarse with centuries,
and mourn bitterly, day by day, my perfect joy.

☽

BROKEN SYMMETRY

*In particle physics, a state in which traces of an earlier
symmetry can be found.*

It's come to this: the corona of that oak
won't mean. Yet once each tree spoke
to me some whispered, wooded truth—
neither joy nor fear but a sentence
of both accompanied by finch and cicada
crazy for love an instant before death.

Gregorian chant first lifted me,
and then stereo, Peter, Paul, and Mary
conjuring the lemon tree, a hammer
to smash injustice, stacks spewing city ash.
Crosses cluttered the landscape, trees
of the knowledge of miracle and demon.

When the snake looped around Mary's feet,
she crushed its head, brought evil to heel
with the holy mumbo jumbo of denial.
Saturday afternoons something unspeakable
would ooze from ocean or Alpha Centauri,
but God or the army would eat it up.

The Baltimore Catechism glued us together.
Why did God make me? To show forth His Goodness.
He was not humble. In high school
the Chemistry Angel spread wings to display
the certainties of the periodic table.
I played with Our Friend the Atom, plastic

smooth as my model Spitfires and Stukas—
no leptons or quarks to clutter the skies.
Life was tidy, the color map of heaven

in the theology book, purgatory and hell
tiered neatly beneath. Hemo the Magnificent
was order, ripples drifting from stones

flung by Grandpa God into the cosmic fishpond.
Physics was the fat bat of Rocco Colavito
arcing toward the pitcher's sweating heart
again and again, my sandlot curve dropping
off the table to catch the black
and jerk high the umpire's right arm.

I posed beneath the backyard plum, dressed
to eat thin crisps of God at the altar rail.
It melts in your mouth—not in your hands!
Now, my sister phones from California.
She's moved out of the Board and Care.
She may be married. She went off her lithium.

Love tastes better than meds, she says.
There are voices wriggling from the book
of poems I sent, and a snake. All night
she's been chopping it up. What science
have I to deny her vision, what comfort
to offer beyond the distant rustle

of the ancient family tree? I see
the blade, the bloody pieces writhing
her floor, as together we dream
a fabric unfaded and unrent, a world
without principles of uncertainty,
the pure green iridescence of the whole.

☾

ON POETRY AS PUNISHMENT

They knew the value of a poem,
those Jesuits in Roman collars,
worn soutanes and sad black shoes
who wished to fashion *Leaders*
of the Catholic Middle Class.

When the demerit cards we carried
in our wallets showed a line
of five black marks, just as
the immortal soul was defaced
by crimes venial and mortal—

long hair, tie forgotten,
animal sounds by which we showed
how close to beast a boy can be,
frog legs hanging from urinal,
as if like us the creature struggled

to emerge into evolutionary light
of bell, book, and candle,
or the quick furtive punch
to the groin of the one
just called to blackboard math—

we had Saturday detention.
This meant a bus and train
and the reproachful dolor
of a mother paying dearly to have me
reach above my class.

Jug, we called this shame—
no one knew why. *Latin Scientific,*
my course of study: Caesar, Virgil,

a virgin goddess, Ignatius, Xavier,
Madame Curie, Watson, and Crick.

Some of us had hopes of medicine—
many of the Irish kids, prosecutor
and then judge—but most were pointed
toward the business world, which
we'd want to conquer for Him,

saving our suburban souls
by investment, diversified portfolio,
wise tithe. The punishment was poetry,
poems to be memorized without error
before a body could leave.

When the frost is on the pumpkin
And the fodder's in the shock,
I'd recite again and again
to myself as hours passed, knowing
the attempt aloud to Prefect

would be heard by the roomful
of snickering, snorting miscreants.
How easily word could get out,
a man condemned to high school hell
for reciting poorly, or too well.

Ay, tear her tattered ensign down!
Long has it waved on high,
and *A wind blew out of a cloud,*
chilling My beautiful Annabel Lee.
Feet of muddy trotter plodded

across the page, pulling me
in the sulky of adolescence.

Hoary verse, but still a new language
too human for me to be content
with all the other ways to say.

Later, as I waited by the tracks
for the Rapid Transit to rumble
the future to me, the poems
waited too, and have remained,
not penance, but a way to labor

this life. By word and song
we say our failing, cry our pride,
fields we've left fallow or crops
gotten in before the frost,
timbers of Old Ironsides gory red

or lapped by harbor tides,
youth's beauty pale and dying
on the bed beside the desk,
lines we work to know by heart
and measure out the distance of a life.

☾

SPRING PICNIC WITH NEWTON,
SUDDEN STORM

Corpus omne perseverare,
Newton begins his Law of Inertia.
Every body perseveres until some force

intervenes. Every two bodies, ours
together now twenty years, four limbs
signing the alphabet of marriage.

Now lighting reveals it all,
electricity from Greek *electron*
from *amber*, resin oozing out to seal

the moment of us. Time has been, will
be our intercourse. *Careless love,*
you sing, moving with me in extremis.

Like prayers we said as children,
O Jesus, O please, the will's triumph
of near helplessness. So passion

becomes us. We set a world in motion
and translate a million wild leaves,
pliant shagbark shattered by storm.

Thunder rouses us. We run to the car,
laughing, put lips together, tongues.
So we understand. So we persevere.

☾

YOUR DREAM HOUSE

Must see to believe.

April raises green scaffolding, builds on each lot
a teeming house of life. Winds bear the savor
of caulk and stain, unearthed earth, lush new cement,

incense of varnish, curlicued thews of maple.
Squirrel and chipmunk scrabble up shagbark hickory
in neighborhoods secured by flagstone, asphalt.

The air fills with hammer and saw. What lives
lays down its scent to mark a place. A headline
announces *National Private Property Week.*

Signs sprout on chemical lawns. Realtors, fresh from
courses at the tech college, immaculate in frosted coifs
or checkered sport coats, white belts, and shoes,

wait in open houses for The Sale. *Sell the wife,*
they've been taught. *The husband will come 'round.*
Papers are rustled, offers countered, pens flourished,

maps to the treasure sketched with letters of a name,
given and family. *A House Is Forever,* the banker swears,
and every saver aches to own, to put down roots.

Close by in the cemetery, mealy leaves swirling
in great vortices, on a patch of lawn a backhoe
kept at bay all winter begins to growl, lifts head

and bears shiny fangs. Workmen struggle with spring
to erect over the foundation a green tent large enough
to house one shattered family, one last rite.

☾

THE RECKONING

The last days, pages
of the rarest book,
flutter down
from these familiar trees.

Awake alone, I'm auditor
of my petty past,
certified accountant
poring over the books.

I'm Samuel Pepys,
confessing furtive lusts
to his diary, *Elle*
being mighty jolie,

or any Puritan father,
ladderback-stiff
on New Year's Eve,
calculating sanctity

on a musty ledger
of piety and misdeed,
though I'm not predestined
to end in the black.

How often I've come
short of what's right,
inaction's ease rather than
the charge of crusade.

Here's life's summit,
year 40, but I'm placed
by the doctors I frequent
somewhere between *Well,*

thank you and *Not at all.*
Memory spirits me away
fast as that Rapido train
from Milan to Calabria

on which I met a woman
who laughed arpeggios
through my bones,
dark and lithe architect

from Venice, cenotaph
of all art, whose dream
was to see the L.A.
she knew from American T.V.

Always that searching
for some place memory
hasn't raised the flag,
some way not gone.

This sinning would go on
forever, I once thought.
No matter how I tell it,
abacus or rosary beads,

I'll come up short—
so much remains
uncollected and untold.
The best I can hope for,

semi-invalid half-life,
calls from that sycamore
igniting with another day,
one blaze of redbird

high enough to trill
all Ohio from despair.
I can't quit now.
I'm dying to hear

the last words.

☾

HOMAGE TO THE UNDERTAKER

Even before my first baby clothes,
it was measured to fit my adult limbs alone,
a serious suit, pressed in front
but wrinkled where I'll come to lie.

The shoes already are laid out, shined
bright enough to return the degree
of wonder and grief to each who'll come near,
soles to stay unmarked because all the way

I'll be given a ride. White shirt,
appropriate for this world and the next,
and at my throat a sober tie,
flawless knot hiding the plastic clip.

No need for wallet, wristwatch, keys.
From the hour I began to wonder,
I've wanted to know when I'll be called
to be dressed this last time,

somebody else's masterpiece of fashion,
bloodless work of perfect art,
on my eyelids and lips until the end
of flesh the fingerprints of strangers.

☾

THE DANCING OF THE BEES, THE PROGRESS OF MULTIPLE SCLEROSIS

By their wraggle-dance,
fluid loops and whorls
they make in air,

they tell the others
of the sweet riot of light
blooming just beyond

their lives, and map
the way. Hours
he's envied their flight

as his hand has labored
its meaty weight
across the radiance of page.

☾

THE HOUSE OF PAIN

The old Greeks tried to flee
unending nights of ache,
agonies like blade on blade,
by hiding in rented rooms
in the Temple of Asklepios,

but pain is a haunted house
that reads our mind. *He
has seen but half the universe,*
Emerson says, *who has not
been shown the house of pain.*

Here some drafts only disturb,
but others suck our breath,
make us sweat each heartbeat,
or frost windows bone-white.
Such nights, desire is nothing

but desire for nothing.
Muscles spasm, backs crack.
We bark shins on table legs,
singe fingers at the grate,
chairs too heavy—nearly.

Kant was able for one night
to will away his pain,
five loud toes of gout,
by sitting close as he could
to the fire and studying

the speeches of Cicero,
but Kant, after all, was Kant.

For most of us, if pain
chains and locks us in,
we will study no one else.

☾

I sit before this keyboard
debating whether to tell my mother
in my dutiful-child letter,
along with granddaughterly triumphs

and devilishly clever meals
I've devised for wife and kids—
news to make her beam (so I
can see her beaming as she reads)—

the sentence from the MRI report
the doctor intoned over the phone,
a bone-cold, unthinkable thing:
There is evidence of cerebral atrophy.

Twenty-five years an adult; still
I worry. She'd take it personally,
remembering a day she worked
too hard, ate or drank something

her Louisiana landlady-witch said
would twist the baby's mind,
a night she loved my father
hard enough to hurt my head.

I could be inventing reasons
more cogent for yes or no
in this debate were my brain
not ceding territory, the M.S.

causing *atrophy*, meaning what—
my college Greek so far gone—
a lack of food? It *is* a hunger,
this damn darkness, lesions

like weeds; I'd been promised
a field of light to last a life.
I decide to decide about Mother
next week. I try to find a poem,

conjuring that remote country
of passion and panic I think I own.
Stars come out to stay.
A thing learned never leaves.

A mother is a young woman always,
starlight in her hair styled
from films that never fade,
seams straight on new hose

as she steps into clouds of steam
from a train just arrived
in New Orleans from Cleveland,
the handsome second lieutenant

surprising her from the side
with a breathless embrace,
a fist of perfect fleshy roses.
Wartime, but no one screams.

Such fervent caring, pairings.
There is no distance between
the alluring fictions our memories
can be and brutal truths,

between a poem of starry trains
and a letter of uninjuring love,
bone and the heart's flesh,
a mind and all it can feel.

☾

PROGNOSIS

Approximately 40%–50% of MS patients develop a subcor-
tical dementia.

—S. M. RAO

What are the odds in this struggle
between what I'll never know
and what I know or might discover
but will come to forget?
An endurance race, stroking

through the Sea of Dementia.
On days like this I fear
I've already begun to sink
from the weight of virus and gene
and myelin sheathing flaking

from cells of spinal cord and brain.
I could pray to be saved
at the last moment by early death,
or even—why not say it,
considering the miracle

of fundamentalist proportion
it would take, in spite of
the Calabrian ancestors who warn
that to say a hope is to sink it?—
a cure. But will I know when?

Well, yes. No. I don't know
whether or not I'll be aware
of the incremental loss of knowing.
Gödel's Incompleteness Theorem
insists that a system—even one

as cocksure as the brain can be—
needs a space beyond itself
to know. The Grand Unified Theory,
were we ever to discover it,
would need something outside—

an element beyond all things,
as it were—to prove it true,
keep it floating. Can I think
what it would be like
not to be able to think,

or even to think less well?
The ideal, it occurs to me,
would be to grow more demented
at the exact rate at which
the physical features of the disease

progressed, an equilibrium of sorts,
though on a downward scale,
as if a swimmer's fatigue,
accelerating slowly, were matched
by a corresponding progression

in the intensity of the storm,
so it wasn't until slipping
beneath the mad waves for good
that he noticed a difference
in what he'd felt had been

a steady progress toward shore,
and thus his last strokes,
as spastic and spasmodic as
they might appear to those watching
helplessly from the beach

as the storm came up, dark
and confusing, nevertheless
caused him no panic,
no desperate regret for all
he'd had to leave undone, but

a bliss blossoming like morphine,
benign, mind-humming ignorance
like the belief that every day
in every way he was getting
better and better, which

would be preferable, I think
now—having just come
from an appointment with
the bright young neurologist,
her eyes averting mine,

who seems to know so much
of the future we share—
to the sorrow and shame
I might have felt thrashing
about for the sake of the ones

who'd pulled for me and prayed
all along I'd make it
as whole and sound as the one
they'd always known, ones
I've known less well, I know now,

or think I do—though I may come
at last to change my mind
or have it changed
for me—than they were owed
for the wager of their love.

☾

II.

SMELLING THE SNOW

THE OTHER WHITE MEAT

Modern breeding techniques have so altered the physical properties of the pig, he is often unable to achieve intromission without manual assistance.

So it's this far our hungers
have herded us troughward,
a grievous mortal weight
hauling its awkwardness.

Jowls, grease-slick tongue,
heart laboring to dance—
all for that fleeting satiety,
happiness that can't last.

Our nurturing brother,
still able to get up
now and then to wallow toward
desire, can't enter paradise

no matter the loud hours
he blubbers and grunts,
a snorting, bruiting snout.
He needs a hand, the very one

that feeds him only to be
fed. O Improbable Largeness,
magnificent obscenity,
must our gluttonies lead us

to frustration, belly flop
of longing that won't cease
until will itself is hammered
or shot between the eyes?

Show us what becomes of one
raised to greed and slaughter,
a sacrifice to no god but wanting,
love's elimination.

☾

"Large Bear Deceives Me"

—Chippewa death-song

Not only the telegraphed blow
massive as Ursa Major,
raking claws, teeth roaring
like falling rock or hail,

it's also by chicanery
the bear can make you prey.
An uncloudy day he drops
purring where you kneel

to your reflection afloat
on lapping stream, or
bides his time in the corner,
looming up where you lie

rolled in those night-furs
of dream you'd known since
the womb as sanctuary,
where you thought the world

couldn't find your scent.
You don't think? He's there,
taps one shoulder only
to appear at once at the other.

Younger, you think sinew, speed
will keep you whole, but age
makes you dread his panting,
the canny subterfuge, steals

your breath when you ache
to make a chant of healing or joy
one note longer. Beware.
He could turn even a song

against you, rearing suddenly
as you open wide as night
to life's final surprise,
the sweet delicate meat of you.

☾

FIREFLIES

Not flies at all, but beetles,
a field flowering in darkness,
the nighest stars, dancing.

Lampyridae, the Greeks said,
shining fire. Even Aristotle
was blinded by the very idea.

A child, I could believe them
to be angels who didn't fall
to blazes but landed on earth.

Flickering names, love-codes
above the dark topography,
small glints of what might be

floating over what is for now,
a brilliance in the eyes
of children who'll grow

to forget, except now
and again, how even a creature
this delicate and small

can find a way through
acres of ravenous night
by its own insistent light.

☾

THE PRACTICAL ORNITHOLOGIST

We listen to the birds
even more carefully
now that all the angels—
Powers, Dominions, Thrones—
have been exterminated,

because, despite shotguns
cocked and cradled,
herbicides encapsulated
to last all season,
they survive, thrive even,

because, despite gashes
of strip shopping centers
and acres of malls,
they continue to say
nothing but what they are,

such candid chanting
charming our hearts,
and because, for those times
when charm fails,
they can escape us

by moving out of range
in the line of fright
or, in swelling circles,
become so much higher
than we hope, traversing

light-strewn heavens
and stars like swinging bells,
and, because of all

their travels, notes
that shatter skull walls

as we lie silent in sleep
or love, stirring
to their angelic music,
we think they know things
that, if only we knew

them too, we could lift
from our heavy days
into cloud, leaving only
trembling air and the one
true song of our lives.

☾

THE ART OF HUMMINGBIRDS

Milkweed-light they hover
above the border
between the nations
of August and December,
their tiny hearts
a faint and frantic thunder.

Night's out of the question,
sightless blight
of eternal hibernation,
but then stamens unfurl
the windstrewn light
and pistils fashion

a day's infinity of seed.
Gardens are hours,
deepest fields
a matter of weeks,
life a desperate quest
for its own essence and hue.

To create another day
each hummingbird
must discover
before this light dies
and brings an end to dreaming
at least one thousand flowers.

May the art of our own lives
be to strive
a thousand times a day
for some utter beauty
beyond us and all around.
May we achieve such perfect need.

☾

CLOWN FISH

When the female dies,
the father of her offspring
changes sex and mates
with the nearest male.

Some grief sweeps us away.
We struggle back into
a strange new ocean,
magic with what we've lost.

☾

ON THE PROPOSITION THAT A NATION GETS THE CUISINE IT DESERVES

> *. . . the Calabrian larder, a meager one. I have read that it has*
> *been enriched on occasion by storks and eagles, but this I fear*
> *I am unable to confirm.*
>
> —WAVERLEY ROOT, *The Food of Italy*

I learned when I was old enough
at table to listen and taste
that the *bel canto* passion of the family,
beating, rippling wings of flight,
could enhance the simplest meal.

Laughter, outrage, or other joy
concerning this still-new land,
crazy as Calabria but grand
as dreams of cash and love,
and at least one adult a meal,

face Chianti red, would throw
the napkin down, stalk off,
glasses of wine and water
and the eyes of children
vibrating with each receding step.

To eat was to know what to think.
Fish meant God had died,
but once a year salted cod,
baccala, was some wondrous birth,
gifts of *torrone* and *panettone*.

I'd break my haunted fast
with dawn prayers and crusts
of bread in steamy milk

and a little bitter coffee,
to reverence the ancestors.

At noon, it was insults.
From lunchbox would come
the salami or *melanzan'*
and the hoots of fairer boys,
last names of *O'* or *-ski.*

They'd hold their noses
at the grated pecorino Romano,
call me *Guinea, Dago, Wop—*
but this was America, so
they too had new names.

Sunday dinner, garlic cloves
glistened in olive oil
like wedding petals, darkening
to church-wood until
music filled our every room.

Even hunks of bony gristle,
fatty strings of stewing hen,
and sausage like fire
aged hours in bubbling tomato
spiked with basil, parsley.

Around the simple table ritual
where always there's room,
and even a bitter laughter
erupts like wild birds,
there can be no poor fare.

☾

YES, THEY HAD NO TOMATOES

As he carries in two hands
from noon's profusion of garden
a tomato ripe this moment,
warm as a lover's whisper

from the pendulous August sun,
breast-heavy promise of a new world,
bruiseless fruit to brood over,
he wonders again how

in the gleaming blue bowl
of the Mediterranean world
the Greeks, Etruscans, Romans
could grow wise, sloe-eyed, mighty

without knowing the tomato.
Other missing treasures
from America he understands
they could do without,

potatoes, chilies, chocolate—
stolidness, urgency, pleasure.
But a day of summer sun,
an age with no tomatoes!

☾

CHILI

Those ruddy ones knew you
as the magic word to scream
headache away, and gout,
to suck pain from phantom limb.

Tomato's meaner sister—
not pepper, as lost Columbus
thought, but nightshade's
tongue cutting deep enough

to take the mind off.
The moral flavor, we bite
through your skin to be
granted brief leave to think

of times we've hurt
with sharp word, until roaring
sweeps over the prairie,
killing thought, all salt,

bitter, sweet. Glowing coal,
bit of hell, green defiance
of desert, you go evening-red
at noon to grow corn's gold.

No cold water, tequila, beer
can help us now, burning oil
spattering the mouth.
Bread may help but not too soon.

A ration of passion or anger,
a match flaring us home
to the body, teary sting
of mortality, our wounded tongue.

☾

POTATO

The lowly potato.
Incas told time
by what it took to cook.

We toll our moments
by oven, skillet, pot—
the wait for soft.

Conquistadors
brought it back to Spain,
holy dowdy charm

potent enough to firm
the limp or ease
the recalcitrant to love.

Could they even dream
they were feeding us
the future? The rich

flung them at the poor,
who, because a spud
endures all weather

with its peasant coat
and yields more calories
per acre than grain,

dug in, clinging to
the yielding dirt
of home, mud or loam,

and opened mouths
to a modest sacrament,
our buried inheritance.

☾

Real Man Delivers an Anti-Pastoral to the Columbus, Ohio, Chamber of Commerce

It's not in cities I won't be myself,
these days of nature's selfish whine, the call
to put, above progress, a hoot-owl's health.
A manly heart fears no cholesterol.
The proper name of love's *Metropolis*,
where asphalt toughens tender lungs and feet,
and rubber tires careen us like a kiss,
and newsprint takes our fingerprints, sweet heat
of scented flesh beneath Armani suit.
Besides, show me a sky as yet unpalled.
Developers reap every field, the loot
of clear-cut timber, acres brightly malled.
   This ecosystem's had its way too long:
   We have dominion. Who's to say we're wrong?

☾

FAT POEM

Late in the Paleolithic, before

this sumptuous ease, because the first need was *Flee*,

beasts stayed lean. Life was thin, *Chase, make haste.* We ran

and hid for our few good tastes, the breast, a fresh kill steaming

the hard, inhospitable stars. Now, a billion hens laying their stoned days away,

fetid feedlots deep with DES and marbled prime, hogs too gross to breed

without helping human hands, neurotic calves penned to the dark, what

we ache for, *Crave, crave,* because of what we used to be

and what we are, is good enough

to break our hearts.

☾

The War between Cookbooks and Diet Books

We grow fat. We grow thin.
The writings of the dead
sustain us. At a Thai funeral,
an act of love: a book
of the corpse's favorite recipes
is presented to family and friends.
The cold tongues of kin dance
with our own. Grandma
bakes our sweet cakes,
then she expires. We stir
sauces with heirloom spoons.
Daddy's garden blooms, withers,
blooms, withers. It's a war
between hot and cold,
cookbooks and diet books.
Mothers smile and frown,
clutch their hearts
and urge us, *Eat, eat.*

☾

SMELLING THE SNOW

I've heard it said
there are those on such
close terms with night
they can smell the very light.

Not only does the moon,
they say, give off a scent
nothing like the sun's,
but old moon smells

sweeter than slivered new.
Monks of old claimed sin
took the breath away, while
God was wild onion, lilac, pine.

I know a carpenter who
boasts he can sniff out a maple
in a woodlot of ash and oak.
A stalking cat knows

the unsinging sparrow
from the finch. This day
as it returns to Ohio, like
some feathery creature

seeking the very moon and tree
where it was born,
I can smell the snow,
which seems to me,

against the dark trees
moving in slow procession,

a few birds stark and silent,
an essence close to love.

But any old fool can smell love.

☾

III.

THE EXCOMMUNICATION OF THE LOCUSTS

Sister Mary Appassionata Chases the Wind

Walk out into this industrial wind
and it hits you: we're eroding.
Even the light is dirty.
We can't tell what is or isn't us,
immune systems growing confused.

Think of Pandora's nasties wafting
like rotten pollen on the thermals,
fanged angels with bat faces
flapping above Egypt's nurseries,
ill winds blowing everybody bad.

It's not that we've not tried
to stop it. Ethiopians sliced
at the wind with shining knives.
Eskimo women swung clubs
to chase bony cold from the hearth.

Herodotus praised the African army
that marched into desert
behind cymbal and drum
to drive away deadly drought,
but it lured them on, turned

on them, and now they lean at rest
in the sandstorm of forever.
Pliny the Elder thought it
the breath of stars
until Vesuvius burned his ass.

Tonight it shakes the moon,
brandishes oak and ash at heaven,
Orion lurching like a drunk,
the air bright knives, warnings,
the winds of angry angels.

☾

Sister Mary Appassionata on the Excommunication of the Locusts

In Paris, a cock swollen with pride
forgot his place and committed
the *Heinous and unnatural crime against
God and man of laying an egg.*
He was bound to the stake and burned,

the pungent scents of the sentence
teaching the poor a truth
concerning the unappeasable appetite
for crisply executed justice
of those who cling to power.

Cows and sows and ewes who'd allowed
themselves to be sweet-talked
by lonely masters, positioned above them—
or behind—by the Master-Maker,
suffered the lash, lost their heads.

Hungry mosquitoes, horseflies,
locusts and weevils and bees,
even man's best friends, who'd let it slip
their minds that they were fashioned
but to serve, were excommunicated.

A sow appeared in 1386 before
the Falaise tribunal, and counsel
provided by the court argued with success
that since both swinish and human hungers
were created by the all-wise Master,

there'd been no sin, unless He—the He
Who Made Us—had made a mortal mistake.
Still, she'd eaten a human baby,

a sin if ever there was one,
so the sow was sternly lectured

by the judges—firmly officious
in flowing robes and scowls—who told her
that while she'd overstepped the bounds
even of beastliness, she'd have gotten off
if she hadn't given in to this yen

on Friday, on which the Savior
has suspended His decree of our dominion
over beast and fowl, and ordered
*This day thou shalt not put teeth
to meat.* The sentence was capital.

After a priest heard her confession
and administered chrism and holy water,
she was tortured, then held in a cell
with the worst of her human peers,
fed on the finest swill at public expense,

and hanged with full ceremony on the square,
such rite serving as eloquent deterrence
to any beast who had thoughts of
yanking the great chain of being,
putting, before the horse, the cart.

☾

Sister Mary Appassionata Announces the Winning Project in the Eighth-Grade Science Fair: Our Good Friends the Insects

A bug for every ailment, so
we lovers can go on forever.
Royal jelly keeps a body light;
not one beekeeper in the history
of honey has known impotence or gout.
Mosquitoes can draw out paresis,
final throes of V.D., and give
curable yellow fever in return.

Only King Roach ever was, will be.
Even earthworms are D.P.'s,
our natives having been iced
by glaciers, the newcomers sailing
in potted plants of Pilgrims.
Burrowing into prairie and bog,
they loved themselves until they came
to eat and excrete a continent.

Termites, ants, swarming gnats
can be baked in tasty cakes,
but let me recommend our special:
tender grasshopper nuggets.
Chinese ladies kept cicadas
in dainty jade cages, chewed food
for them, dished out on porcelain,
slept to love's timeless chiming.

At night, spread a muslin cloth
around an ash that smells of mice—
their scent. Shake the branches,
and the iridescent beetles, too cold

to flee, will drop from heaven
like manna. Hippocrates found
that, ground, they cured dropsy
and scratched a thousand other itches,

but every teen knows *cantharides*
as the Spanish fly that can
make a man feverish enough to force
a groundhog hole or ironwood knot,
drive a woman so mad she'll try
Oh, the big fat candle of desire,
breathless, *Oh,* wild ride,
the knobbed gearshift of love.

☾

Sister Mary Appassionata to the Chamber of Commerce: Remains of Earliest Hominid Discovered in Ruins of Atlantis under Lake Erie

Imagine your lost daughter,
lips glaring like refinery flares,
crack rocks and douche bottle
heavy in her purse, coming on

to pillars of the community
on a neon street. *Hey now,*
Mister, knees of hose ruined
as she kneels, slow rhythm

of hand and head, up, down,
before an idling BMW, up, down,
gulp of bitter poison,
the awful groaning stillness.

We're killing her, you see?
Or your grandmother, gumming
the hard wad of Doublemint
she found under a potted plant

at the glorious Galleria
before she was booted out,
lying under cardboard before
the AmeriTrust atrium.

Or your own Appalachian mamma
in day-glo pasties, back
still stiff and proud
in the honky-tonk mirror

as she humps the disco pole,
her kids in mortal fear
of the boyfriend back home.
Goddesses of our cities.

Atlantis, she's another story:
state of the feminine we
knew enough to worship
long away and far ago, pure

as hoarfrost beyond the suburbs,
no citizens whining, *But
how much will a just world
cost us? How damn much?*

*O City Fathers, on Public Square
let us float municipal bonds
and build an underwater park
to honor her, trees, a statue*

*anatomically correct, a plaque:
Here lies Mother. On this spot
the Goddess wound up our sexes
like bedroom alarms and set us off.*

*She lies untarred by the lake
of commerce, slough of this
our daily effluent. Let us
resurrect her by moving as one,*

*our caring for one another
the one prayer she'll hear.
Let us heed her cries, moans
of double-helixed generation*

whorling from her pretty shell,
passion's splash and ooze,
love honest and equal,
water music, heart's blood.

☾

SISTER MARY APPASSIONATA EXPLICATES A GRAFFITO FOR THE EIGHTH-GRADE BOYS

Don't look up here for a joke.
It's in your hand.

Little old man wearing a rain hat.
He's got a mind of his own:
stands up to anything, but
finding home, he cries and cries.
Lies down and dies.

Stings, then like a drone
expires just to sweeten the honey.

So damn polite. He bows,
loyal family retainer minding
his manners, but suddenly
a puppet Punch chasing each Judy.

When you must be chaste?
Foams like a mad dog.

The old snake in the grass,
but holier than thou
the morning after, burning
from every indiscretion.

After all, he's your life.
And he'll be the death of you.

Time after time he rises
from bed faithful as dawn,
as if love were
the only mortal reason
to say to night *Not yet.*

SISTER MARY APPASSIONATA, MARRIAGE COUNSELOR

Constancy is for the birds: 92%
twitter and flit the joys
of the faithful married life.

Mourning doves, e.g., pair off
till Death do they part,
hoot out matins and lauds

in crack-of-dawn duets,
bill and coo on wires running
taut above the two-lane

the blessings of staying put.
But in the teeming barnyard
a single gobbling Tom

will strut through scores
of moaning, lovey-dovey hens.
Flushed female chimps breathless

with estrus choose to stoop
before all male comers;
and a whole day's worth

of frantic chest drumming
by the hairy bull gorilla
can't keep his ladies

from climbing other trees
to peel forbidden fruit.
So go figure. The Creator

wishes us to keep all but one
field fallow, or wants us
to sow some wider, wilder oats;

or, chaste and single forever
yet having a son with an eye
for the ladies, He can't decide,

and this uncertainty makes
history, the scorecard of love,
our world of joy and woe.

☾

SISTER MARY APPASSIONATA ON THE HISTORY OF MADNESS

It all began in water.
Diodorus of Sicily discovered
the African lake whose waters
bubbled through souls of those
who drank, making them babble
every sin they'd hid,

and Pliny's spring in Asia Minor
loved by Apollo, its chill
driving bathers crazy enough
to know all things
but too much knowing dragging them
like lead to the oozy bottom.

The man who disrupted Mass
by lifting skirts of devout maidens
during the elevation of the Host
was no lunatic, though
Thomas More had him flogged
to teach what passion costs,

believers caught too often
with heads in cloud and bodies
immersed in the elements,
hell flaring from frictions
of heart and soul, divine match
struck on rough-hewn human stone.

In Germany, the Dancing Mania,
perjurers held right hands raised,
fingers of the left crossed
as they danced and whirled.

Adulterers lay writhing, moaning
on bellies and backs, every position.

On June 26, 1428, a monk
driven by the demons of loneliness
began to dance, and when he'd used up
every inch of his cell, he died.
Even a timid mystic is aberrant
in this bloody literal world.

When we conceive too narrowly,
nothing connects. Orson Welles
proved what the ancients knew well,
that looking up on an uncloudy night
can make the soul confuse
the truly beautiful and true.

Faith is the essence of insanity,
Paul knew, all that's hoped for,
everything unseen. If we ache
only for what is, we're nothing
but the torn-winged wren
fluttering near time's fierce cat.

☾

IV.

Curse of the Mummy's Tomb

THE GIRL WHO MADE THE STARS

—after a Bushman tale

She reached down with both hands,
scooped the ashes, flung them high,
a touch of grace for all the pain.

Like this she tossed them, singing
Ashes, ashes be our Milky Way.
Blow through night from one end

to the other. Be to us every dream,
wonder, all the mystery we can eat.
Glow the people home at night for love.

Stand for our very true, our not.
She is my mother, the girl who made
the stars, the woman who told me

her mother told her this, her rage
at drafts a blessing like maple smoke,
her body all the time in the world,

that face branded into everything
I ever will remember, drifting with
the wind, those charred, scarred hands.

☽

New Poem

It all begins
with dawn, bedclothes
feverish and damp.

The chafed swelling
ticking slowly, slowly
down, fathers

like cinema wolfmen
becoming themselves
again. Mothers

cover aching breasts,
nipples tender
and raw, ragged breath

subsiding, a shiver
sweet and trilling
all day long

whenever they cross
their legs. A dog.
Flurries of birds.

And the children
step out into light
and run for their lives.

☾

GATHERING THE DEAR SWEET DEAD

Some nights, walking
into wind alone, I
can feel them on my eyes,
riffling my hair like

a mother's sigh, those
who walked this way before,
breathed, loved
or at least died trying.

They whisper and hiss,
tremble from trees
to scrabble and scurry
across concrete as I pass.

I stop, stoop. Dry
as fine paper, smooth bond,
one more face and name,
one more faint scream.

☾

A BRIEF SOCIAL HISTORY OF SPIT

Unless it comes with fervent kiss—
baby's, lover's, trusty mutt's—
it disgusts. In *Sophists at Dinner*,

Athenaeus tattles on piggy Demylos,
who glistened dishes he wished no one else
to taste. Erasmus ordered students

to grind theirs underfoot so as not
to distract vellum-dry scholars
from their labor, his classroom passion

spraying the first two fearful rows.
At medieval meals it was thought rude
to stain the wall nearest the table.

The rich were taught to use linen
if they wanted to impress, but alone
or, just as good, among the poor,

who had little more than thatch,
patches, and the shirts on their backs,
of course the floor would do.

I'm told an old Nonna christened me
because dark had made my brothers dry
as beans, and still Calabrians let fly

at evil eyes. *Don't blow on your food,*
my mother would say. *It's crude.*
Never a wind without some rain.

When I put aside sandlot ball
with other childish things,
I lost the fluidity of speech

which defies even August thirst,
shut my mouth on a repertoire
of spritzies, drizzlers, hacks

by which I thought a real man
said his name, marked his place.
What was it for but to cure blindness,

to express that we are dusty dirt,
soon to be smeared and washed away
by unpredictable heaven?

Youth is free, we say with our mouths,
to tell the world, if ever
so briefly, I am, I was, *here.*

☾

MEDITATION ON THE THREE FORMS OF TONGUE PROTRUSION

—after Desmond Morris

1. THE TONGUE OF CONCENTRATION

Maybe I see it, way back in mists.
I'm a swaddling gurgle, the *Primo*,
firstborn son the neighborhood beats
a path to, sated at last, bringing
a new mind to the task of pushing away
the stiffened nipple. Or the sandlotter
struggling to master the curve, stride
shortened, middle and index fingers
snapping down, thumb up, as if
I tried to dance back the scarlet line
on the thermometer so Mother wouldn't know
I shouldn't play. One night
an opposing coach, who'd studied me
from the third base box for three innings,
his batters beginning to know exactly
what I was about, told me that if
the intention was to go places
on the sinew and whip of my hard left arm,
"You'll have to learn, son, when
you throw the bender, to keep
your damn tongue in your mouth."

2. THE RUDE TONGUE

A sign to Sister, her black back
turning on some new humiliation of ours,

cosmic or petty, some insistence
that in every gesture and word
she had the unleavened truth right there
in her mouth, melting slow as history.

3. THE SEXY TONGUE

This one, my darling, you—
swollen lips wetted by fever, hands
twisting white above you
on the headboard—know already,
you writhe of curves,
small cries as I concentrate
on the craft of our rude passion,
my devotion a taste too true,
older even than speech,
this mortal tongue of love.

☾

FRA LIPPO LIPPI INVENTS A NEW HALO

You understand me: I'm a beast, I know.
—ROBERT BROWNING

Was this some sadistic bishop's joke,
assigning you in the fading hues
of middle age to the convent at Prato?

At matins, candle flames like stars
about their heads, the young nuns, lips
like sweet peaches, sought forgiveness

for the bodies men had convinced them
were sin, beauty leading to the grave.
Lucrezia Buti came of age in the fire

of your gaze as you stammered what
little Latin you knew, her body teaching you
eternal things. It was inevitable,

I suppose, the anonymous denunciations
to the Office of Monasteries and the Night—
Vasari says Lucrezia and five other nuns

moved into your house. Prodigious appetite,
this addiction to beauty, but what
woman or man who viewed your angels

or the Madonnas that still chill the flesh,
beings of this world modeling the divine,
the loveliest lies in lapis and gold,

would be shocked at the beast of beauty
you became? The comic self-portrait
in *Madonna and Child with Saints and Angels—*

you watch us as we gaze, and the head
of the bloody Baptist served up at table,
hating the sinner even as you loved the sin.

There was other imperfection—you never
could draw hands—but your new halo,
translucent shimmer of the holy space

a body takes, grand dance of human rites,
no art but what in a lifetime we can dream
better, conceive, proportion, color, love.

☾

A Matter of Perspective

In *Madonna and Child with Saints and Angels*
Filippo Lippi's figures grapple with rapture
before, to either side, and far behind.
The portly artist himself leans in to spy
on the holiness breaking out everywhere.

Lifeguard angels in Donatello's *Assumption*
flex and preen in marble to swoon Mary,
pretty feet and knees peeking at us.
Quattrocento wanderlust of the eye.
Childhood was a 3-D View-master.

I could see just short of forever,
and pored over lapis and gold trappings
of holy card cathedrals. Art was to adore
from a distance, fine, dolorous ladies,
bleeding, thorn-pricked hearts,

but belief in sight unseen grew old.
A down-to-earth virgin appeared in ecstasy
on the very bed where my parents
had brought me into relief beneath stares
of the family dead. We assumed lives,

put ourselves in some perspective.
To the old artists the distance between
light and dark was the lie we pretend
is not. We move about in distances
we invent, architecture of wishing,

the soul's geometries patterning us,
flights and sleights of hand

to try the eye, heavenly falsehoods,
belief in the space art takes up.
Without beauty the world is flat.

☾

THE BOTTOM LINE

The relationship of which the painting is the deposit was . . . a
commercial relationship.

> —BAXENDALL, *Painting and Experience*
> *in Fifteenth-Century Italy*

Borso d'Este, Duke of Ferrara, knew so well
what he liked that he bought his art
by the foot, 10 *lire Bolognese* per sq. *pede*,

while Giovanni de'Bardi, businessman
who understood the value of taking pains,
endowing all his artist's time, still insisted

on the art of the deal, nailing it down
in writing. Whether the patron's wealth
comes from usury or birth, art is for sale.

The world will pay to make beauty's truth
the bottom line. Working my simple arias,
I entertain little thought of cash—

though *Poetry* pays by the line.
The university, prim, grudging, grim
in stony ivy, breathes over my shoulder,

taps her foot and color-codes my fate
in triplicate. Tenure in this world
of artlessness, respect I ache to earn

from those I'd love: payment enough
to dance hand across canvas or page,
but the real reasons for such submission

can't be itemized. The commission begins
with a gaze tentative at first, colors
slow but running to the vanishing point,

moral geometries of relation, vision
line by line, a contract between
the self and the rest of the world.

☾

Coach

All my life I've known yet not
known him. By *him* I mean not
the Little League martinet who drank
more than a bit and put ice
in my bones when he'd grab
my arm hard and let me see
the red years of not-quite in his eyes
and screamed at me not to hit
off the back foot or stick out
my tongue when I concentrated
on gripping the curve across the seams,
or in high school
the sex education teacher and line coach
who preached while wearing both hats
the same evangelical message,
You can beat the other man, Citino,
if you work harder and smarter than
he does and *When the going gets tough*
the tough get going,
and *It's not the size of the dog*
in the fight it's the size of the fight
in the dog, or later one
of his bigger Big Ten brothers
who quoted Emerson on moral reason
but once on the sidelines
during a bowl game punched
an opposing linebacker in the face,
or another who puts a box of Tampax
in the locker of the young man
he feels isn't going full-out
in practice, or the one
who whines on the radio call-in show,
The cupboard was bare when I
got here and tells the Rotary

at lunch, *We got too many slow*
white guys this year.
It's not any one coach, really,
but the kind of man whose life
becomes so purely circumscribed,
rendered simple by buzzer or bell,
lined diamond, rectangle, square
to *Where in the goddam hell were*
you going on that play? or *Hit*
somebody. Take his head off,
the kind of man for whom
time is a grim and dire game
and the soul only a shallow channel
for anger gushing out of nowhere
and every childish idea, the kind
of man I sometimes fear I am.

☾

Whole Wheat, Decaf Black, a Morbid Curiosity

We study the paper, fingers darkening
with the stinking ink
of daily news,

as Daddy bangs Mom's head against
the bedroom wall, the thuds
like night thunder,

as baby is shaken until
the crying stops, and silence
reigns again,

as the sniper's scope
X's-out another tribal enemy,
all for ethnic cleansing,

as boys in street colors
redden the shirts of other boys
with rage, semiautomatic,

as village women bind the girl,
legs spread, cut the pearl
from its precious shell

so she can know holiness.
It's not that we worship blood,
as the ancestors did—is it?

Somewhere, someone knows
a suffering too terrible and loud
for words, nearly.

Thank God it's not us.

There but for fortune—
but give us the details.

What was she wearing?

☾

In Bavaria, Two Vietnamese Beaten
by Skinheads while Onlookers Cheer

I'm stopped at a light,
given that brief leave
to rattle sheaves
of my own little history
that such interludes bring,
not of course prepared
for anything like horror,
but a car, nondescript
and unmarked, flies by
and the driver salutes me
smartly, obscenely,
in the Nazi way, and before
I can think anything but
a thin siren of outrage
I see I'm wrong,
the man was only adjusting
the rearview mirror
and I breathe,
I breathe, I breathe.

☾

COLD, COLD POEM

At our age, this heat!
Two bodies inflamed as one.
And a voice on the radio—
Temperature down to zero.
Bitter cold out there,

and I wonder, as we lie here,
sweat mingling, why *bitter?*
Why not *sour, sweet,* even,
like the close odors down at
the Open Shelter on West State

below the banks, the men
in their cavernous room drifting off
after macaroni, bread, beans,
thinking of women who
once or twice were kind,

while nearby the women dream
of men who come home sober
with fat paychecks,
rich scents of labor
in their hair and clothes,

to sit with the children
at the kitchen table,
pots boiling noisily
on the stove, the oven
ticking its generous heat.

And I understand. We say
cold is bitter because
it makes us grimace, as if

on the wind we tasted blood,
salt, our own death.

Homelessness is utter cold,
the numbing ache
of being kept outside
while others feast, nights
of nowhere, sleeping alone.

☾

At the Well-Endowed Museum; or, Curse of the Mummy's Tomb

1.

This Western leisure grows lethal,
creature comforts of the New Age aging us
before our time, skin blackening
with tabloid ink, hearts growing hard.
I stand in the Egyptian antiquities room
of the Cleveland Museum of Art
before the same painted sarcophagi
that turned my lips cold when
I was last here, a child on a field trip
from Ascension of Our Lord School
to the Land of the Dead. I think
of the artisans, painters, sculptors,
especially the cutters who labored
airless shifts in the Valley of the Kings,
years measured in blood and rock,
bitter sweat and beer
and the desperate pride of craft.
They hollowed out mountains with soft chisels
for priests who had persuaded the pharaohs
they'd live a lovely forever
without brains, livers, spleens—
sad little sacks of wizened flesh,
eternal raisins, shriveled puds.
How the workers must have smirked,
laughter rising like stars,
for all the ache in skull and back.
Where are the grand painted tombs where
these artists lie, regal, bejeweled?
I would travel there.

2.

Howard Carter's pet canary, eaten
by a ghostly cobra after Tut's violation.
Lord Carnarvon, struck down by an avenging mosquito
sentried in unguent-stained dark.
The very moment Carnarvon died, lights
went out in Cairo, and in England at Highclere,
according to a hundred banner headlines,
the lord's favorite dog howled at the moon
and perished. Others were lost as time
snatched them, pale, eminent Egyptologists
across Europe and the U.S.
stricken by the grimly wrapped avenger
as they worked, ate, loved.
And in San Francisco, a guard working
the traveling exhibit had a stroke
while on duty before the treasures
of the magnificent Tut.
His estate sued the city.

3.

The curse was a hoax, of course, made
of the adult lust for lost mystery;
but in Egypt, the boy-pharaoh
led a revolution which chilled
governments of the West,
filled streets with those angered
at rising tides of crime against
the poor dead of the poor nations,
felonies against culture,
piggish collectors who dragged off
stelae, figurines, statues, mummies
to airport and train station.

Now, generation after generation,
they while away the Sunday afternoons
of eternity in climate-controlled cells
in Cleveland and a hundred other cities.
Tut, at least, made it back to Egypt.
For the modern West it becomes
harder and harder to find wonders
for sale. The Valley of the Kings
is now threatened by overdigging,
especially of the minor tombs,
by American archaeologists desperate
for tenure in their universities.
Soon there will be no stone upon a stone,
nothing of the dead left to eat.

4.

They made an art of leaving, the Egyptians,
and I am more haunted by the discovery
that this room in the museum
has not changed from my childhood than I am
by the realization that the artifacts
have endured forty centuries.
Did I ever expect that my life,
flesh stretched across
brittle, unaged bone,
would transform these monuments?
It is more, I think, than fearing
my own dissolution. Perhaps
I can learn to love the dizzying sweep of it.
Sick to the heart, the immune system,
unmortally wounded, wrapped
in my own numbness, I've changed
terribly, wonderfully in the forty years
since I last visited this cool, sealed place,

imagining the dying lives
of Tut, Rameses, Seti, and the others
for whom the noble laborers
bring down hammers
on blunt chisels, making beautiful rooms
deep in rock for treasuries
of light, dragging out in baskets
millions of tons of rubble
to be replaced by hollow bodies
of stiff and fragrant and immortal gods.

☾